Fashions for the New World Order

Fashions for the New World Order

More Cartoons by Pat Oliphant

Andrews and McMeel
A Universal Press Syndicate Company
Kansas City

Oliphant ® is distributed internationally by Universal Press Syndicate.

Fashions for the New World Order © 1991 by Universal Press Syndicate. All rights reserved. Printed in the United States of America. No part of this book may be used or reproduced in any manner whatsoever without written permission except in the case of reprints in the context of reviews. For information write Andrews and McMeel, a Universal Press Syndicate Company, 4900 Main Street, Kansas City, Missouri 64112.

ISBN: 0-8362-1879-5

Library of Congress Catalog Card Number: 91-73165

June 4, 1990

5

June 7, 1990

AGENDAS.

ONWARD TO THE PROMISED LAND.

FREE SPEECH ON TRIAL IN THE GREAT HALL OF THE PEOPLE: DJO BI DEN PRESENTS HIS AMENDMENT, WATCHED APPROVINGLY BY DENG XAIO BUSH AND LI PENG DOLE.

'HERE'S MY NUMBER,' SECRETARY BAKER TOLD ISRAEL. 'WHEN YOU DECIDE YOU WANT TO BE SERIOUS ABOUT PEACE, CALL.' THEN HE SAT DOWN TO WAIT.

DONALD TRUMP'S BANKERS.

THE SACRIFICE.

'LOOKING FOR THESE, MR. PRESIDENT?'

COMMUNIST PARTY 28TH CONGRESS.

THE URUGUAY ROUND.

'DID ANYONE BOTHER TO CHECK MR. HUBBLE'S PRESCRIPTION BEFORE HE LEFT?...OH, WHAT THE HECK...'

GREAT S&L MOMENTS: NEIL BUSH ABASHEDLY REVEALS TO THE BOARD OF SILVERADO THAT HE IS, INDEED, NONE OTHER THAN THE SON OF PRESIDENT GEORGE BUSH.

'CAN YOU DIRECT ME TO THE CAMBODIA POLICY SECTION?'

July 25, 1990

VANILLA.

34

THE SEARCH FOR JUDGE SOUTER.

'MR. STEINBRENNER — MY, WHAT AN UNEXPECTED PLEASURE!'

'YES, IT'S AN ARAB THING, BUT WHY SHOULD WE GET INVOLVED?'

'WELL .. SO FAR, SO GOOD.'

DISCONCERTING ARAB CUSTOMS: ACTUALLY, YOU HAVE NOTHING TO FEAR. YOU ARE HIS GUEST.

TICK, TICK, TICK...

'ALL SET, CHIEF, WE'RE GONNA BRING ON THE ANCHOR. NOW, JUST BE YOURSELF, ANSWER THE QUESTIONS AND BE AS INFLAMMATORY AS YOU CAN...'

'IT'S THAT COP AGAIN, TRYING TO SELL US TICKETS TO THE POLICEMEN'S BALL!'

September 6, 1990

'WE'VE BEEN HERE TOO LONG — THEY'RE STARTING TO LOOK GOOD.'

THE WALL.

'THE DRESSING FOR SCHOOL IN ARMOR, THE TEARFUL FAREWELLS, ALL THAT IS VERY DISCONCERTING, BUT THE YELLOW RIBBONS ARE A NICE TOUCH.'

'THANK GOODNESS YOU'RE HERE, DR. ASSAD — HELP ME CONTROL THIS MONSTER I CREATED!'

'ONE MORE LITTLE GAUNTLET, JUDGE SOUTER — THE SENSITIVITY TEST.'

THE HAZARDS OF A NEW YORK CITY EDUCATION: PART II

'IT WON'T WORK. FIRST WE'LL GET A DEFICIT, A RECESSION, INFLATION AND UNEMPLOYMENT, THEN EVERYONE WILL START QUIBBLING ABOUT THE CAPITAL GAINS TAX.'

'OH, HELMUT — YOUR RELATIVES ARE HERE!'

BAD DAY FOR MOTHER HUBBARD.

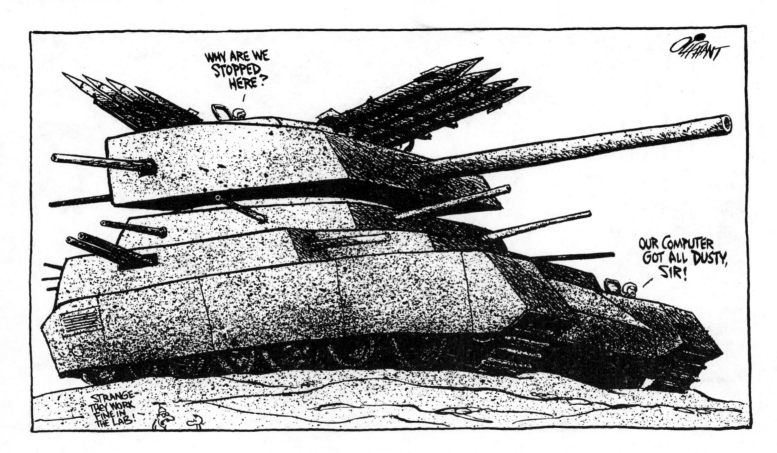

TO GEORGE BUSH, THE 1990 DEFENSE SPENDING, ECONOMICS AND CIVIL RIGHTS NOBEL PIES.

THE PRESIDENT HELPS THE CANDIDATE.

HOG WALLOW, 1990.

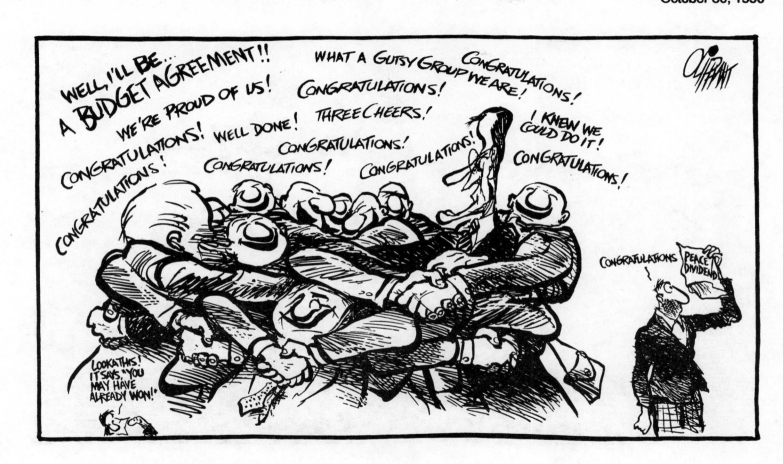

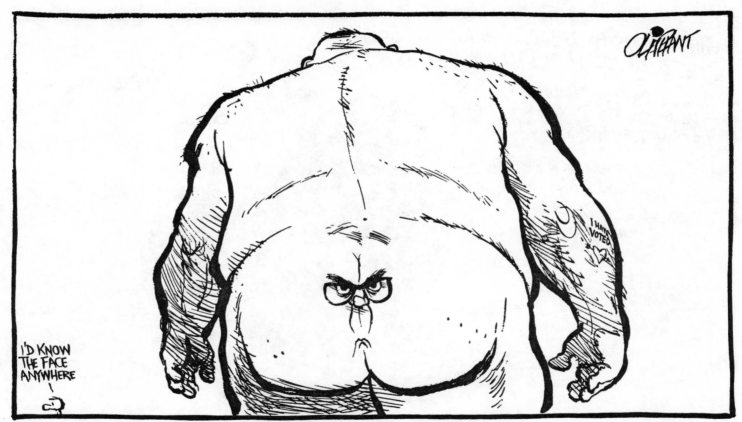

CONSCIENCE OF THE CAROLINAS.

'AN AMERICAN SUCCESS STORY, CHAPTER ONE: CALL ME RONNIE...'

'KEEP IT DOWN, YOU GUYS—I CAN'T HEAR A 'DAM' WORD NORIEGA'S SAYING.'

'..SO I CALLED THIS NEWS CONFERENCE TO GET ALL OF OUR MID-EAST POLICIES OUT IN THE OPEN.'

'OH, WELL, RULE BRITANNIA! ONWARD TO VICTORY, AND ALL THAT!'

DRIVING MIZ THATCHER.

'WHY YES! A RECESSION! I BELIEVE A RECESSION IS INDEED A POSSIBILITY!'

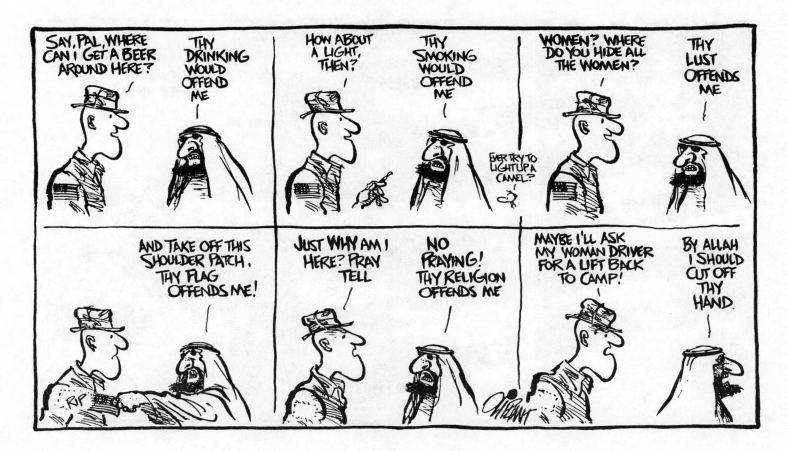

December 7, 1990

'WELL, I GUESS WE'RE ALL SET FOR THE HOLIDAYS — THE TREE DECORATED, THE PRESENTS IN PLACE, A NICE WREATH IN THE WINDOW, MOM AND DAD IN THE DESERT...'

STILL THE BEST CONGRESSIONAL TERM-LIMITING DEVICE.

'WHAT'S THE FAILURE RATE WITH THESE THINGS?'

'THOSE WERE THE DAYS! JOE STALIN — THERE WAS A **LEADER**, BY GOD!'

ON THE HOME FRONT, THE PRESIDENT ACTS TO STEM THE EVIL FORCES OF POVERTY, DRUGS, HOMELESSNESS...

'HOME, WIFE, GREAT JOB, TOP MAN IN MY FIELD, DYNAMIC LEADER, WORLD ADMIRATION, NOBEL PEACE PRIZE — MAN, I HAD IT MADE!... THEN I BLEW IT ALL ON MY COMMUNISM HABIT.'

A TOUCHING CONCERN FOR CIVILIANS.

'THIRTY THOUSAND FOR DINNER LAST NIGHT, FIFTY THOUSAND FOR BREAKFAST TODAY, EIGHTY THOUSAND FOR LUNCH—IT'S TIME TO CALL OFF THE DAMN WAR!'

YOU'RE ON CAMERA, OFFICER GORBY.

THE GUARDIAN.

A STAR IS BORN.

FOR OUR NEXT ACT,...

April 3, 1991

EGG ACTUALLY SUMMONS SPERM, SCIENTISTS CLAIM IN LATEST FINDING.

NIXON VISITS THE SOVIET UNION.

'ANYONE FOR TENNIS?'

KITTY KELLEY'S LAST INTERVIEW.

WHILE BUILDING A SHELTER IN THE MOUNTAINS, MASSOUD THE REBEL STRUCK OIL. MASSIVE MILITARY AID FOR THE OPPRESSED PEOPLE OF KURDISTAN WILL ARRIVE SHORTLY.

DEMOCRACY OR...   BUST!

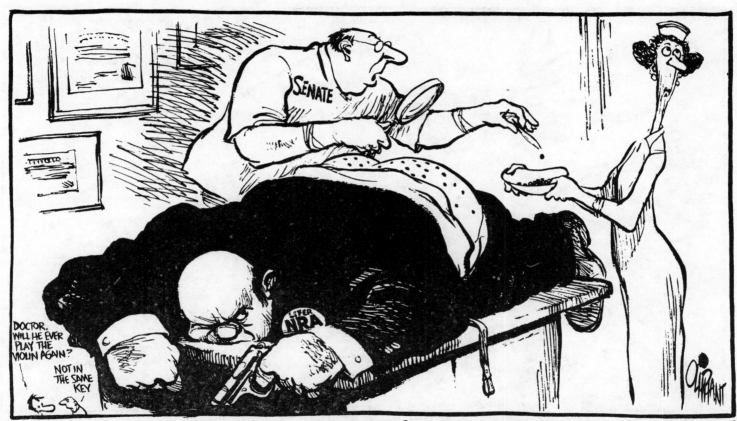

'I GUESS WE CAN SEW YOU BACK UP, BUT THESE GUYS SURE WEREN'T USING A HANDGUN.'

May 16, 1991

140

SOUTER AND SOUTER.

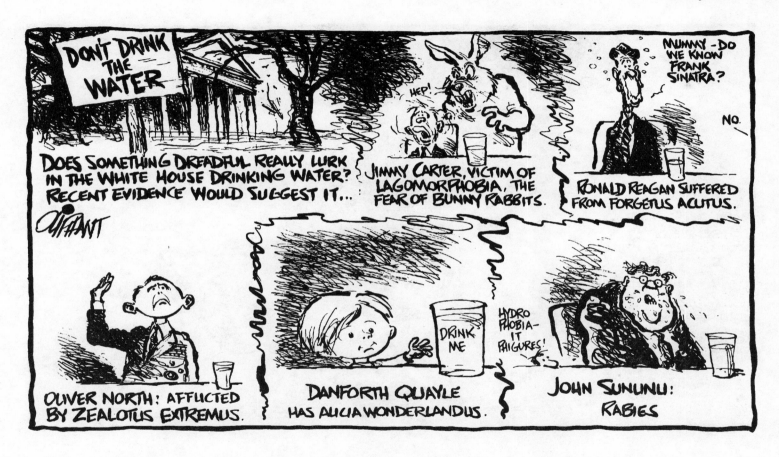

LET THE GLORIOUS DESERT·STORM·1992·BUSH·CAMPAIGN·KICK·OFF·PARADE BEGIN.

'BAD ENOUGH, I SAY, TO HAVE WOMEN ORDAINED IN THE FIRST PLACE. NOW, WHAT WAS ALL THAT ABOUT ORDAINING SOME LEBANESE WOMAN? WHAT?'

June 12, 1991

'NOW, DON'T TAKE ANY GUFF FROM HIM — WALK IN THERE, TAKE THE SOUP LIKE HE OWES IT TO YOU, AND WALK OUT AGAIN. HE'LL PROBABLY WANT YOU TO STAY AND SING, BUT JUST TELL HIM TO GO TO HELL!'

DRIVING MIZ THATCHER (CONTINUED).

'LONG LIVE THE GLORIOUS SOVEREIGN STATES OF GREATER ZUG AND LOWER SLOBENIA!'